WOMEN IN STEM
JANE GOODALL
GROUNDBREAKING PRIMATOLOGIST

by Clara MacCarald

Ideas for Parents and Teachers

Pogo Books let children practice reading informational text while introducing them to nonfiction features such as headings, labels, sidebars, maps, and diagrams, as well as a table of contents, glossary, and index.

Carefully leveled text with a strong photo match offers early fluent readers the support they need to succeed.

Before Reading

- "Walk" through the book and point out the various nonfiction features. Ask the student what purpose each feature serves.

- Look at the glossary together. Read and discuss the words.

Read the Book

- Have the child read the book independently.

- Invite him or her to list questions that arise from reading.

After Reading

- Discuss the child's questions. Talk about how he or she might find answers to those questions.

- Prompt the child to think more. Ask: Did you know about Jane Goodall before reading this book? What more would you like to learn about her work or about chimp behavior?

Pogo Books are published by Jump!
5357 Penn Avenue South
Minneapolis, MN 55419
www.jumplibrary.com

Copyright © 2024 Jump!
International copyright reserved in all countries.
No part of this book may be reproduced in any form without written permission from the publisher.

Library of Congress Cataloging-in-Publication Data

Names: MacCarald, Clara, 1979- author.
Title: Jane Goodall: groundbreaking primatologist / by Clara MacCarald.
Description: Minneapolis, MN: Jump! Inc., [2024]
Series: Women in STEM | Includes index.
Audience: Ages 7-10
Identifiers: LCCN 2023033243 (print)
LCCN 2023033244 (ebook)
ISBN 9798889967019 (hardcover)
ISBN 9798889967026 (paperback)
ISBN 9798889967033 (ebook)
Subjects: LCSH: Goodall, Jane, 1934–Juvenile literature. | Primatologists–England–Biography–Juvenile literature. | Chimpanzees–Behavior–Tanzania–Juvenile literature.
Classification: LCC QL31.G58 M33 2024 (print)
LCC QL31.G58 (ebook)
DDC 599.8092 [B] –dc23/eng/20230801
LC record available at https://lccn.loc.gov/2023033243
LC ebook record available at https://lccn.loc.gov/2023033244

Editor: Katie Chanez
Designer: Emma Almgren-Bersie

Photo Credits: Danita Delimont/Alamy, cover (foreground); zahorec/Shutterstock, cover (chimp); Shutterstock, cover (background); Tinseltown/Shutterstock, 1; Eric Isselee/Shutterstock, 3; United Archives GmbH/Alamy, 4; Chendongshan/Shutterstock, 5; Viacheslav Lopatin/Shutterstock, 6-7, 9; Jonathan Blair/Corbis/Getty, 8-9; CBS Photo Archive/Getty, 10; guenterguni/iStock, 11; Everett Collection Inc/Alamy, 12-13; Steve Bloom Images/Alamy, 14-15; Nature Picture Library/Alamy, 16-17; Neil Aronson/Shutterstock, 18; Adrian Warren/Mary Evans Picture Library/SuperStock, 19; Michel Gunther/Science Source, 20-21; Chansom Pantip/Shutterstock, 23.

Printed in the United States of America at Corporate Graphics in North Mankato, Minnesota.

TABLE OF CONTENTS

CHAPTER 1
A Love of Animals 4

CHAPTER 2
Among the Chimps 10

CHAPTER 3
A Champion for Animals 18

ACTIVITIES & TOOLS
Try This! 22
Glossary 23
Index 24
To Learn More 24

CHAPTER 1
A LOVE OF ANIMALS

Have you ever watched animals? What **behaviors** did you see? Jane Goodall studied chimpanzees. She discovered they could do amazing things.

Jane was born in London, England, in 1934. She grew up around animals. Her family had dogs and cats. She also had a pet bird, hamster, and tortoises.

CHAPTER 1

Jane loved reading about animals, too. She especially liked books about African animals. She wanted to work with them.

Jane did not have money for **college**. She worked many jobs. She still wanted to go to Africa. A friend had a farm in Kenya. Jane decided to go there. She earned enough money for a boat ticket in 1957.

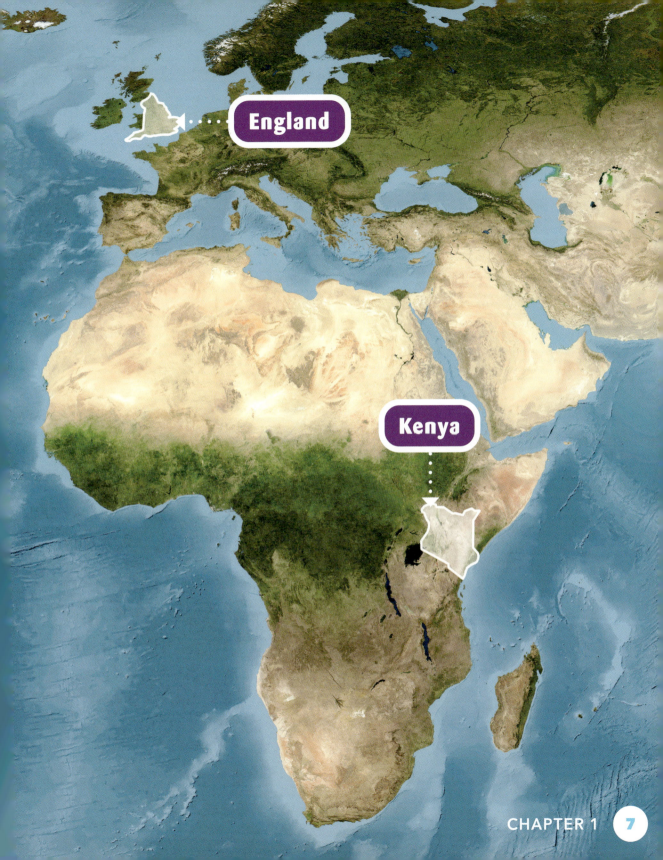

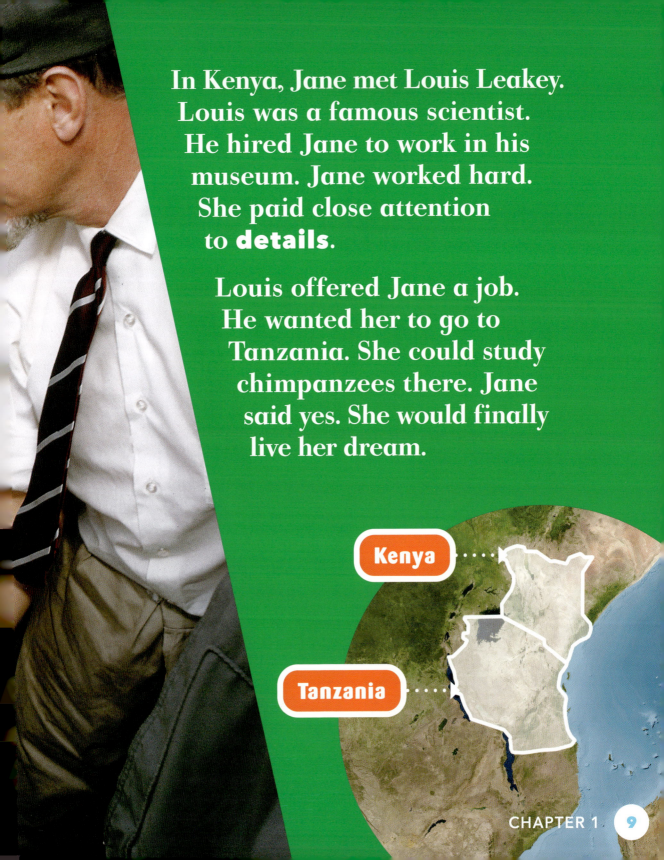

In Kenya, Jane met Louis Leakey. Louis was a famous scientist. He hired Jane to work in his museum. Jane worked hard. She paid close attention to **details**.

Louis offered Jane a job. He wanted her to go to Tanzania. She could study chimpanzees there. Jane said yes. She would finally live her dream.

CHAPTER 2
AMONG THE CHIMPS

Jane arrived at Gombe Stream **National Park** in 1960. She lived in a tent. It was hot. Bugs were everywhere. The forest was thick with plants.

Jane looked for chimps to study. But the chimps hid from people.

CHAPTER 2

Jane did not give up. One day, a chimp walked into her camp. Jane named him David Greybeard. He stole a banana. After that, he let Jane watch him. Soon, the rest of his group did, too.

Jane started learning about chimps. She saw they formed strong **social bonds**. Mothers were loving and patient. Chimps held hands. They **groomed** each other. They had their own personalities. Some were brave. Others were shy.

DID YOU KNOW?

At first, Jane fed the chimps and touched them. Later, she realized this changed their behaviors. It was better to just watch.

termite mound

At the time, scientists thought only humans used **tools**. But Jane saw something amazing. David Greybeard used a stick as a tool. He used it to get **termites** out of a mound.

TAKE A LOOK!

Chimps have different ways of making and using tools. Take a look at one!

❶ The chimp plucks leaves off a stick.

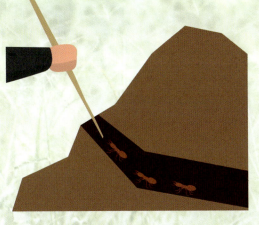

❷ The chimp pokes the stick into a termite mound.

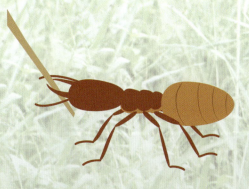

❸ Termites attack the stick. They bite it.

❹ The chimp pulls the stick out and eats the termites.

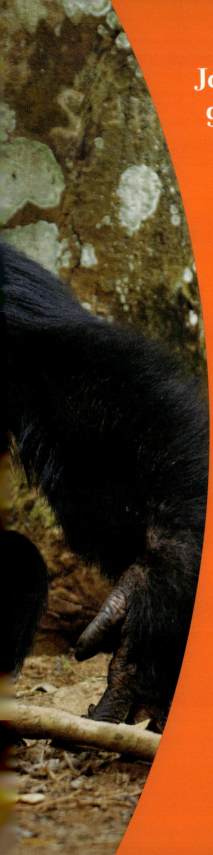

Jane saw chimps use sticks to get honey from beehives, too. They also used other tools. Some used rocks to break open nuts.

DID YOU KNOW?

Scientists once thought chimps only ate plants. But Jane discovered they eat meat, like bugs and birds, too. She discovered chimps are **omnivores**.

CHAPTER 2 17

CHAPTER 3

A CHAMPION FOR ANIMALS

Jane's work was **groundbreaking**. She taught others to look closely at animal behavior. Scientists now know that many animals use tools. Sea otters use rocks to crack open shellfish. Elephants use leaves as flyswatters.

People still study chimps. They continue Jane's work. They make new discoveries about chimp behavior.

CHAPTER 3

As of 2023, Jane has been a **primatologist** for 63 years. She has traveled the world. Jane shares her love of animals. She talks about saving animals and their homes.

DID YOU KNOW?

Jane started the Jane Goodall **Institute** in 1977. It works to protect wild animals and places.

CHAPTER 3

ACTIVITIES & TOOLS

TRY THIS!

STUDYING ANIMAL BEHAVIOR

Anyone can study how animals behave. You just have to watch closely. Pay attention to small details. Give it a try with this activity!

What You Need:
- animal videos
- paper
- pencil

❶ Watch a video of an animal in the wild. Feel free to pause or rewatch it.

❷ Write notes about what you see the animal doing.

❸ Look at each action you wrote down. Why do you think the animal did that? Write some theories, or possible explanations, for the behavior.

❹ Watch a video of a different animal. Write down what you see. Compare your notes. Did the animals in the two videos behave in different ways? Why might that be? Write down your theories.

GLOSSARY

behaviors: Ways in which a person or animal acts.

college: A place that teaches higher learning beyond high school.

details: Small parts of individual things.

groomed: Cleaned an animal, particularly its fur.

groundbreaking: New, important, and unlike what has been done before.

institute: An organization that works toward a specific goal.

national park: A large area of land that is protected by the government.

omnivores: Animals that eat both plants and meat.

primatologist: Someone who studies primates, a group of animals that apes and monkeys belong to.

social bonds: Ties between animals in a group.

termites: Ant-like insects that eat wood and live in groups called colonies.

tools: Objects a person or animal uses to do something to another object or to a living thing.

INDEX

animals 4, 5, 6, 18, 21
behaviors 4, 12, 18, 19
chimpanzees 4, 9, 11, 12, 15, 17, 19
college 6
David Greybeard 12, 14
Gombe Stream National Park 10
Jane Goodall Institute 21
Kenya 6, 9
Leakey, Louis 9

London, England 5
museum 9
personalities 12
primatologist 21
social bonds 12
Tanzania 9
termites 14, 15
tools 14, 15, 17, 18
watched 4, 12

TO LEARN MORE

Finding more information is as easy as 1, 2, 3.

❶ Go to www.factsurfer.com
❷ Enter "JaneGoodall" into the search box.
❸ Choose your book to see a list of websites.